P9-CRJ-562

EASY
792.024 C 52713

Hewitt, Sally
Squeak and Roar.

EASY
792.024 C 52713

Hewitt, Sally
Squeak and Roar.

$14.99

DATE DUE	BORROWER'S NAME	ROOM NUMBER
APR 2 0	R. Grabinski	M03
	R. Johnson	D5
	M. Delato	D5
	D. Bolt	
	[illegible]	

BEECHER ROAD SCHOOL LIBRARY
WOODBRIDGE, CT 06525

EASY
792.024 BEECHER ROAD
SCHOOL LIBRARY
Squeak and roar.
52713

Get set... GO!

Squeak and Roar

Sally Hewitt

Photography by Peter Millard

Contents

Introduction	2	Bang!	14
Voice	4	Bubble trouble	16
Megaphone	6	Splish, splash, splosh!	18
Footsteps	8	Squeak and scratch	20
Rain and hail	10	Crackle and rustle	22
Flap and rumble	12	Index	24

CHILDRENS PRESS®
CHICAGO

Introduction

Listen! The world around you is full of sounds.
Babies cry, traffic hums and rumbles,
machines whirr, dogs bark,
and rain patters down.

You can fill your stories,
puppet shows, and plays
with sounds, too.

Get ready to roar like a lion
and whoosh like the wind.
Make the sound of rumbling thunder
and flapping wings.
Listen to the kettle bubble
and the fire crackle.

Voice

Get ready

✔ Your voice

. . . Get Set

Try making different sounds.
Can you buzz, hum, growl, and squeak?
Pop your cheeks.
Click your tongue.
What do you sound like?

Go!

Make a spooky sound like a ghost.
oooooooooOOOOOOOOoooooooo!
Roar fiercely like a lion.
rrrrooooOOOOAAAARRRR!
Whoosh like the wind.
wwwhhhHHHOOOoooossshhh!

Megaphone

Get ready

✔ Thin cardboard ✔ Safety scissors ✔ Masking tape

. . . Get Set

Cut out a large circle of cardboard.
Fold it in half and cut along the fold.
Fold one half into a cone shape
and tape its edges together.
Cut an opening in the narrow end
big enough to speak into.

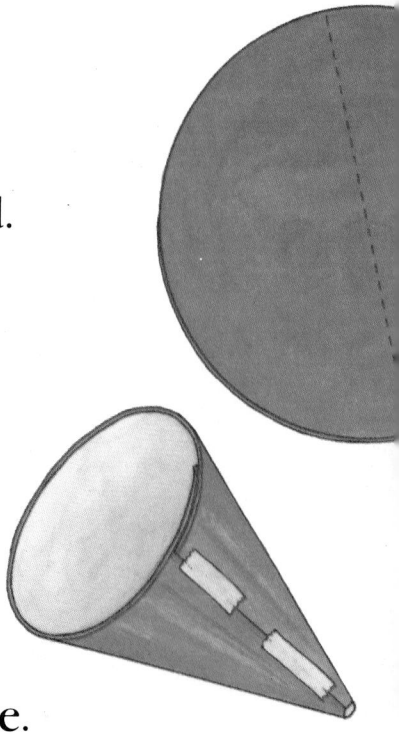

Go!

Squeak, howl, and roar into the cone.
Your voice will sound louder.
Put a crumpled tissue into the cone.
It will muffle your voice and make it softer.

Footsteps

Get ready

- ✔ 2 plastic cups
- ✔ 2 small wooden blocks
- ✔ Cookie sheet
- ✔ Sand or salt

. . . Get Set

Sprinkle the sand or salt onto the cookie sheet.

Go!

"Walk" the 2 cups on a table top and in the tray of sand or salt. Do they sound like footsteps? Now try the wooden blocks. Can you make the footsteps run, jump, and dance?

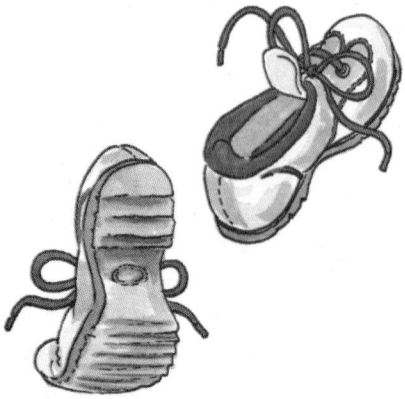

Rain and hail

Get ready

- ✔ Rice
- ✔ Dried peas
- ✔ Colander
- ✔ Cookie sheet

. . . Get Set

Pour some rice into the colander.
Hold the colander over the cookie sheet.

Go!

Shake the colander gently
to make the rice fall through the holes
and onto the cookie sheet.
Listen.
It sounds like pattering rain.
Drop the peas through your fingers
onto the cookie sheet. It sounds like hail.

Flap and rumble

Get ready

- ✔ Small sheet of thin cardboard
- ✔ Big sheet of thin cardboard

. . . Get Set

Hold one end of the small sheet of cardboard.
Hold both ends of the big sheet with a friend.

Go!

Shake and wobble the big sheet
to make the sound
of rumbling thunder.

Flap the smaller sheet
to make the sound of wings.

Bang!

Get ready

- ✔ Square of thin cardboard
- ✔ Glue or masking tape
- ✔ Safety scissors
- ✔ Square of brown paper bigger than the cardboard

. . . Get Set

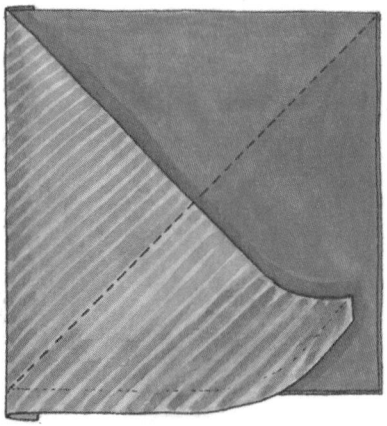

Cut the brown paper in half
to make a triangle.
Place it diagonally
across the cardboard square.
Fold over the edges and tape them underneath.

Go!

Fold the cardboard in half to make another
triangle with the paper inside.
Hold the corner and flick it downward.
The paper will shoot out with a loud bang!

Bubble trouble

Get ready

- ✔ Pans
- ✔ Bowls
- ✔ Bottles
- ✔ Dishwashing liquid
- ✔ Water
- ✔ Long straw

. . . Get Set

Put some water and
a drop of dishwashing liquid
into each container.

Go!

Put the straw in the soapy water and blow.
Do *not* suck the soapy water into your mouth.
Each container makes
a different bubbling sound.
You can make underwater sounds
or the sound of a bubbling kettle.

Splish, splash, splosh!

Get ready

✔ Plastic bottle with a screw top
✔ Water

. . . Get Set

Half-fill the bottle with water.
Screw the lid on tightly.

Go!

Slosh and swish the water around in the bottle.
It sounds like splashing in puddles
or paddling in the sea.
Splish, splash, splosh!

Squeak and scratch

Get ready

- ✔ Shiny plate
- ✔ Sandpaper
- ✔ Plastic bottle
- ✔ Corrugated cardboard
- ✔ Wooden breadboard
- ✔ Cookie sheet

. . . Get Set

Feel the rough and smooth surfaces.

Go!

Wet your finger and rub it hard
on the smooth surfaces.
Listen to the different squeaks.
Make a sound like a mouse
and a creaking door.
Scratch your nails lightly on
the rough surfaces.
Make a sound like sawing wood.

Crackle and rustle

Get ready

- ✔ Tissue paper
- ✔ Aluminum foil
- ✔ Cellophane
- ✔ Newspaper

. . . Get Set

Crumple the different kinds of paper.
Listen to the sounds they make.

Go!

Can you make the crumpled paper
sound like a crackling fire,
a giant munching bones,
or leaves rustling in the wind?
What other sounds can you make?

Index

aluminum foil, 22

bottle, 16, 18, 20
bowl, 16
breadboard, 20
brown paper, 14

cardboard, 6, 12, 14, 20
cellophane, 22
colander, 10
cookie sheet, 8, 10, 20
crackling sound effect, 22

dishwashing liquid, 16
dried peas, 10

flapping wings sound effect, 12
footsteps sound effect, 8

glue, 14

kettle, 2, 16

masking tape, 6, 14
megaphone, 6

newspaper, 22

plastic cup, 8
plate, 20

rain and hail sound effect, 10
rustling sound effect, 22

safety scissors, 6, 14
salt, 8
sand, 8
sandpaper, 20
scratching sound effect, 20
splashing sound effect, 18
squeaking sound effect, 20
straw, 16

thunder sound effect, 12
tissue paper, 22
tongue, 4

underwater sound effect, 16

voice, 4

water, 16, 18
wind sound effect, 4
wooden blocks, 8

Acknowledgments: The author and publisher would like to thank the pupils of Kenmont Primary School, London, for their participation in the photographs of this book.

Editor: Pippa Pollard
Design: Ruth Levy
Cover design: Mike Davis
Artwork: Ruth Levy

Library of Congress Cataloging-in-Publication Data

Hewitt, Sally.
Squeak and roar / by Sally Hewitt.
p. cm. — (Get set— go!)
Includes index.
ISBN 0-516-07995-6
1. Sounds—Juvenile literature. [1. Sound—Experiments. 2. Experiments.] I. Title. II. Series.
QC225.5.H49 1994
792′.024—dc20 94-12309
CIP
AC

1994 Childrens Press® Edition
© 1993 Watts Books, London, New York, Sydney
All rights reserved. Printed in the United States of America.
Published simultaneously in Canada.
1 2 3 4 5 6 7 8 9 0 R 03 02 01 00 99 98 97 96 95 94